WHEN OUR WORLD began, the sea was the only habitat. Then some creatures left the sea to slither, slide, creep, or crawl **across the land.** Finally, some took *flight...*

For Uncle Dave and Aunt Barbara —EGM
For Pauline Greenwood, and in memory of Bart Greenwood —PDG
To Linda —YN

Acknowledgments

The authors would like to thank the following people for their technical expertise:

Laurel Bowman, Greek and Roman Studies, University of Victoria, Canada; Ken Klein, East Asian Library, University of Southern California; Glen MacDonald, Professor of Geography, UCLA; Kevin Padian, Professor and Curator, Integrative Biology and Museum of Paleontology, UC Berkeley.

Special thanks to Dennis Parks, Senior Curator and Director of Collections at the Museum of Flight in Seattle, for his careful review of both the text and illustrations.

INTO THE
AIR
AN ILLUSTRATED TIMELINE
OF FLIGHT

RYAN ANN HUNTER

illustrated by

YAN NASCIMBENE

NATIONAL GEOGRAPHIC
WASHINGTON, D.C.

Book design by Bea Jackson

The body text of the book is set in Stone Serif. The display text is set in Badhouse Bold.

LIBRARY OF CONGRESS CATALOGING–IN–PUBLICATION DATA
Hunter, Ryan Ann.
  Into the air : an illustrated timeline of flight / by Ryan Ann Hunter;
illustrated by Yan Nascimbene.
      p. cm.
Summary: Provides an illustrated chronology of flight, from prehistoric
insects to future spacecraft.
  ISBN 0-7922-5120-2 (Hardcover)
  1. Aeronautics--Chronology--Juvenile literature. [1.
Aeronautics--Chronology.] I. Nascimbene, Yan, ill. II. Title.
  TL547.H81496 2003
  629.13'002'02--dc21

2002154473

One of the world's largest nonprofit scientific and educational organizations, the National Geographic Society was founded in 1888 "for the increase and diffusion of geographic knowledge." Fulfilling this mission, the Society educates and inspires millions every day through its magazines, books, television programs, videos, maps and atlases, research grants, the National Geographic Bee, teacher workshops, and innovative classroom materials. The Society is supported through membership dues, charitable gifts, and income from the sale of its educational products. This support is vital to National Geographic's mission to increase global understanding and promote conservation of our planet through exploration, research, and education.

For more information, please call 1-800-NGS LINE (647-5463) or write to the following address:

National Geographic Society

1145 17th Street N.W.

Washington, D.C. 20036-4688

Visit the Society's Web site at www.nationalgeographic.com.

INTRODUCTION

Getting into the air was a long, arduous process. It took millions of years for first insects, then birds, to take flight. For people, the clues were always close by—those flapping wings, smoke in the wind, the gliding of boomerangs and arrows.

Understanding the clues took imagination, persistence, and courage, as well as advances in science and technology. Finally, it all came together. On December 17, 1903, the Wright brothers achieved powered, controlled, winged flight.

In celebration of humankind's conquest of the air, we have put together a timeline that includes breakthrough events leading up to, and following, the Wright brothers' flight.

We can hardly imagine what new accomplishments lie ahead. Whatever awaits us, people will never forget the first time they soared like birds.

Ryan Ann Hunter

On the timeline, the letters "MYA" are used to indicate "million years ago."

360 MYA

The first millipedes and insects crawled about. Some kinds of insects began to fly.

325 MYA

Giant dragonflies had two-foot wingspans.

210 MYA

Flying reptiles called pterosaurs ruled the skies.

Giant *dragonflies*
zigzagged through steamy swamps
above the heads
of lumbering reptiles.

One branch of the
dinosaurs developed wings.

150 MYA

Archaeopteryx probably couldn't fly as well as today's birds.

125 MYA

Sparrow-size *Sinornis* could fly and perch.

100 MYA

Ichthyornis lived along shorelines and hunted fish.

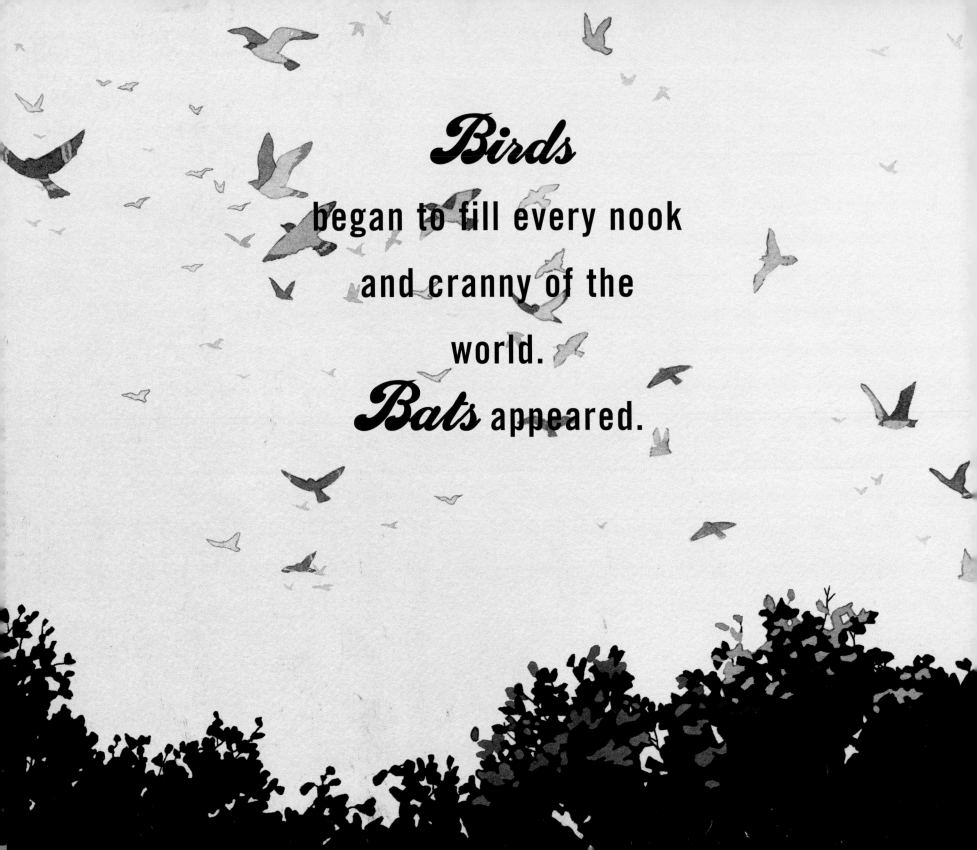

Birds
began to fill every nook
and cranny of the
world.
Bats appeared.

70 MYA

Several groups of birds still in existence today had evolved by this time.

50 MYA

Bats, the only winged mammals, hunted the night skies.

12,000 B.C.

Stone Age peoples fashioned hunting sticks that sailed through the air. These were the first boomerangs.

8000 B.C.

Almost all the bird species we know today existed.

People *watched* birds fly and *wondered* how they did it. Legends told of people flying.

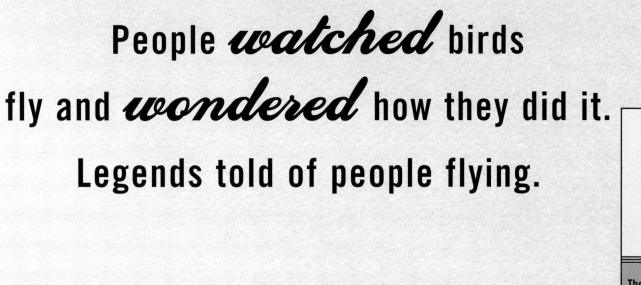

1500 B.C.

The Persian king Kay Kavus was said to have trained four eagles to carry his throne into the air, so that he might invade the heavenly kingdom.

1200 B.C.

According to Greek legend, a boy named Icarus and his father made waxen wings so they could fly. When Icarus flew too close to the sun, the wings melted, and he fell into the sea and drowned.

400 B.C.

Chinese scholar Gongshu Pan supposedly made a wooden, bird-shaped kite that flew for three days.

200 B.C.

Han Xin, a Chinese general, was said to have flown a kite to measure his distance from his enemies. Then he had a tunnel dug to that length in order to surprise his foes from below.

Kites captured the wind and *soared* through the air.

People experimented with homemade wings.

They designed *flying* machines.

A.D. 852

A Spanish scholar jumped from a tower. His oversize garment trapped some air. He made a short, unsteady parachute jump but did not fly.

A.D. 1490

Leonardo da Vinci drew models of flying machines with flapping wings, which he called ornithopters.

A.D. 1010

A monk named Eilmer of Malmesbury strapped on some wings and leaped off a tower. He only broke both legs. Other tower jumpers were not as lucky.

A.D. 1670

Francesco Lana-Terzi thought copper balls would float if air was pumped out. His design wasn't built.

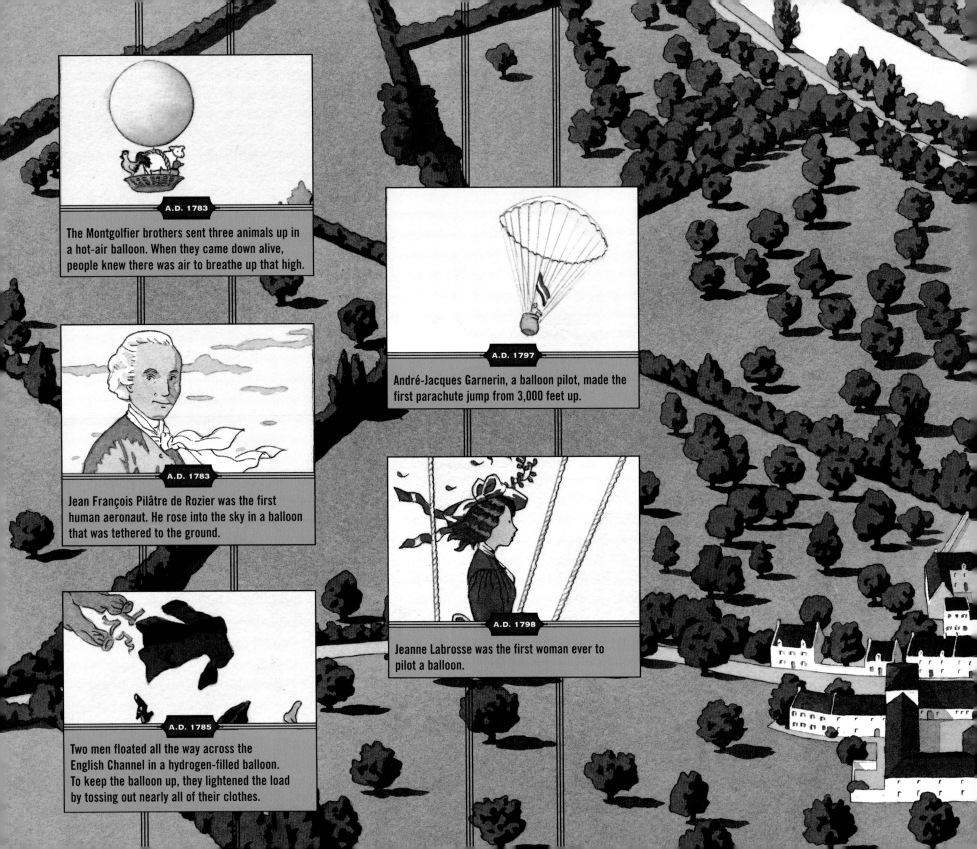

A.D. 1783

The Montgolfier brothers sent three animals up in a hot-air balloon. When they came down alive, people knew there was air to breathe up that high.

A.D. 1783

Jean François Pilâtre de Rozier was the first human aeronaut. He rose into the sky in a balloon that was tethered to the ground.

A.D. 1785

Two men floated all the way across the English Channel in a hydrogen-filled balloon. To keep the balloon up, they lightened the load by tossing out nearly all of their clothes.

A.D. 1797

André-Jacques Garnerin, a balloon pilot, made the first parachute jump from 3,000 feet up.

A.D. 1798

Jeanne Labrosse was the first woman ever to pilot a balloon.

Finally, people did get into the air. But they were *floating*, not flapping.

A.D. 1849

A 10-year-old boy was the first to fly in a heavier-than-air craft, one of Sir George Cayley's gliders. Cayley figured out how birds' wings keep them aloft—what a breakthrough!

A.D. 1852

Henri Giffard set out from Paris in the first passenger airship powered by a steam engine.

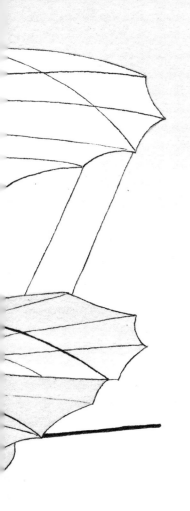

A.D. 1890

Clément Ader's powered aeroplane rose one foot off the ground. But his flight was brief and not controlled.

A.D. 1891

Otto Lilienthal began experimenting with gliders. He made more than 2,000 successful flights before he died in a crash. People remembered his words: "Sacrifices must be made."

Scientists made huge leaps in understanding how the world works. They tried out new *inventions.*

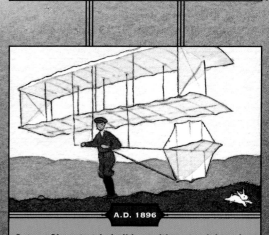

A.D. 1896

Octave Chanute tried gliders with up to eight pairs of stacked wings. He found two pairs worked best.

A.D. 1900

Orville and Wilbur Wright flew their first glider.

A.D. 1907

The first helicopter to carry a person took off. It rose only 5 feet above the ground and stayed in the air for just 20 seconds.

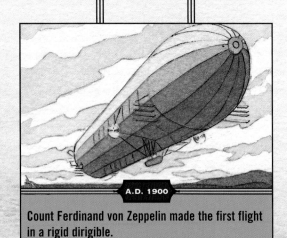

A.D. 1900

Count Ferdinand von Zeppelin made the first flight in a rigid dirigible.

A.D. 1908

Glenn H. Curtiss won the *Scientific American* trophy for the first public flight farther than 1 kilometer (0.6 mile).

A.D. 1903

The Wright brothers took turns in their airplane, *Flyer*. It was the first time a pilot controlled an airplane flying under its own power.

A.D. 1909

Louis Blériot won a $5,000 prize for being first to cross the English Channel in a plane. He had no compass, and mist blocked the sun. Only his instincts kept him from straying too far off course.

The Wright brothers studied
everyone's ideas about flying.
Finally, they did it!
Soon, airplanes *filled the skies*.

A.D. 1910

A Curtiss biplane flown by Eugene B. Ely was the first plane to take off from a ship.

A.D. 1914

The first commercial airliner, a flying boat, took one passenger at a time between St. Petersburg and Tampa, Florida. It landed right on the water.

A.D. 1911

The first flight across America took 84 days. Although the pilot, Calbraith Rodgers, crashed many times on the way, he wouldn't give up.

A.D. 1914

Airplanes were first used in air-to-air combat in World War I.

A.D. 1912

Harriet Quimby was the first woman to fly across the English Channel.

A.D. 1919

Sir John Alcock and Sir Arthur Brown, who had flown planes in World War I, flew nonstop across the Atlantic Ocean and won $50,000!

People raced to go *higher, faster,* and *farther.* Airplanes became a part of everyday life.

What an age of *adventure!*

A.D. 1923

On their third try, John Macready and Oakley Kelly made it nonstop all the way across America.

A.D. 1927

Charles Lindbergh flew solo across the Atlantic and won $25,000. He won more fame than many other record-setters for daring and bravery.

A.D. 1924

Two Douglas World Cruisers made it around the world in 363 hours flying time, but it took 175 days.

A.D. 1929

The dirigible *Graf Zeppelin* went around the world in 21 days, 5 hours, and 54 minutes.

A.D. 1926

Richard E. Byrd, who had explored the Arctic by dogsled, flew over the North Pole in a plane piloted by Floyd Bennett.

A.D. 1929

Louise Thaden won the first American cross-country Women's Air Derby.

A.D. 1932

Amelia Earhart was the first woman to fly alone across the Atlantic Ocean.

A.D. 1938

Hanna Reitsch flew the first practical helicopter inside a Berlin sports arena.

A.D. 1933

Wiley Post made the first solo flight around the world.

A.D. 1939

The first jet-powered plane zoomed through the air.

A.D. 1936

DC-3s were first used for passenger service. The planes were so well built, some are still in use today.

A.D. 1939

The first test version of the Sikorsky helicopter flew. It started the helicopter industry in the U.S.

More kinds of aircraft were designed.
More records were broken.

Then—*faster* than the *speed* of sound!

A.D. 1947

Chuck Yeager broke the sound barrier, flying faster than Mach 1: the speed of sound.

A.D. 1949

A B-50A Superfortress went around the world nonstop, refueling in midair four times.

A.D. 1947

The *Spruce Goose* was the biggest airplane to fly. Its wingspan was longer than a football field! It went one mile at 80 feet but never flew again.

A.D. 1953

Jacqueline Cochran was the first woman to fly faster than Mach 1.

A.D. 1966

The *Harrier* didn't need a runway. It took off and landed vertically.

A.D. 1974

Sunrise II, the first solar-powered aircraft, was launched.

A.D. 1976

The *Concorde*, a supersonic airplane, flew its first scheduled commercial flight, crossing the Atlantic in 3 1/2 hours.

Amid new ideas, age-old *dreams* came true.

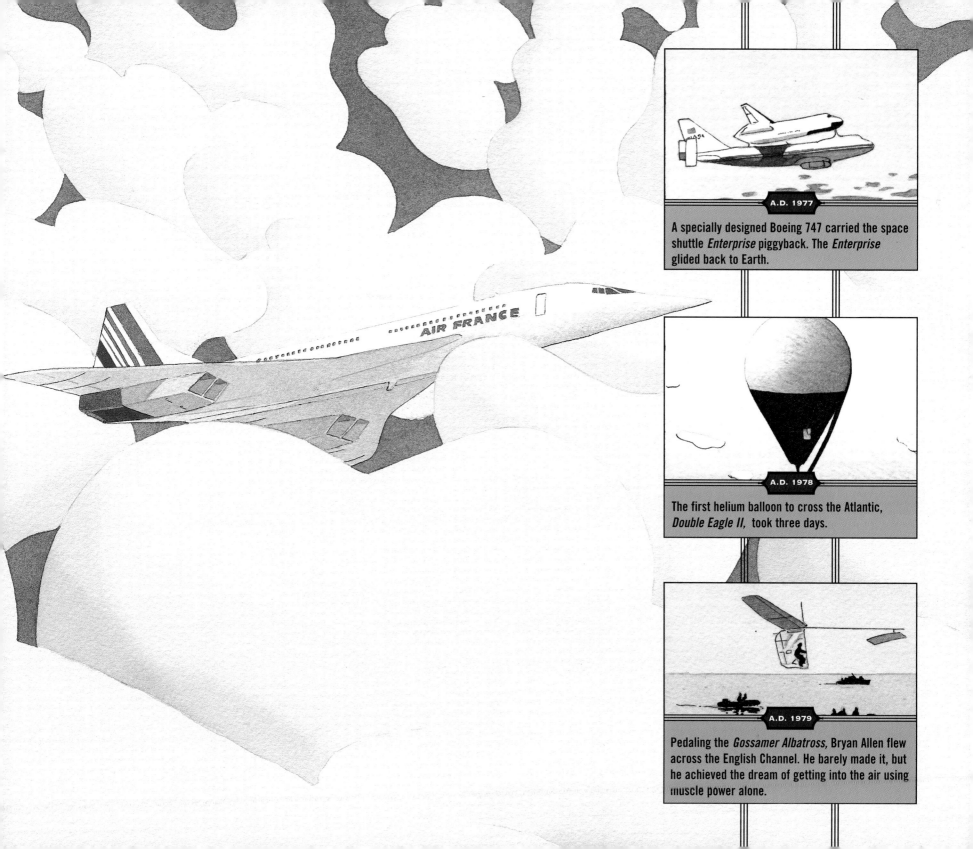

A.D. 1977

A specially designed Boeing 747 carried the space shuttle *Enterprise* piggyback. The *Enterprise* glided back to Earth.

A.D. 1978

The first helium balloon to cross the Atlantic, *Double Eagle II,* took three days.

A.D. 1979

Pedaling the *Gossamer Albatross,* Bryan Allen flew across the English Channel. He barely made it, but he achieved the dream of getting into the air using muscle power alone.

A.D. 1982

The first helicopter to fly around the world was piloted by H. Ross Perot Jr. and Jay Coburn.

A.D. 1994

The first airplane designed entirely on a computer, the Boeing 777, was flown.

A.D. 1986

Voyager, piloted by Dick Rutan and Jeana Yeager, flew nonstop around the world without refueling.

A.D. 1999

More than 200 years after the first balloon ascent, a balloon finally made it all the way around the world.

A.D. 1989

The first Stealth Fighter was used in combat in Panama. Its sharp angles made it hard for radar to detect.

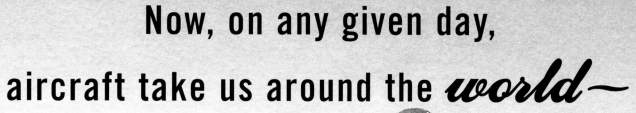

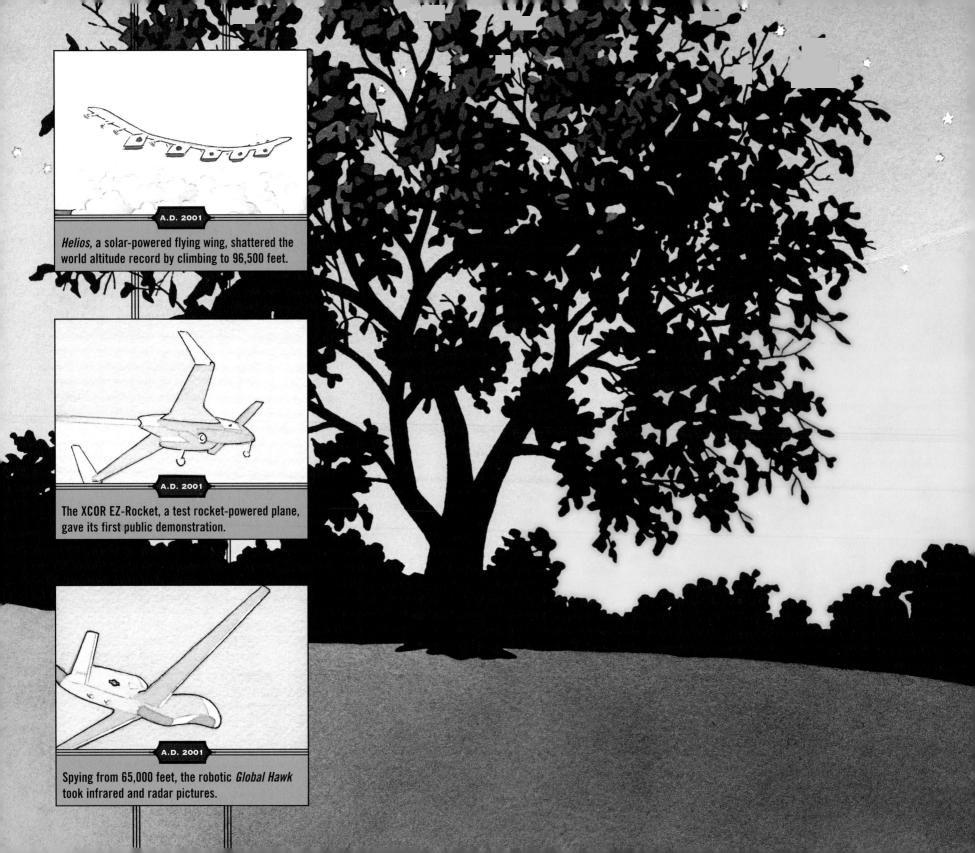

A.D. 2001

Helios, a solar-powered flying wing, shattered the world altitude record by climbing to 96,500 feet.

A.D. 2001

The XCOR EZ-Rocket, a test rocket-powered plane, gave its first public demonstration.

A.D. 2001

Spying from 65,000 feet, the robotic *Global Hawk* took infrared and radar pictures.

and *beyond!*

FUTURE

A double-decker megajet, *Airbus A380,* will carry more than 500 people.

FUTURE

Hypersoars may go as fast as Mach 5. Around-the-world trips will take just two hours.

FUTURE

Spaceplanes might take off from a runway on Earth and land on the moon.

Endnote

Although it took a long time for people to make their first simple trips into the air, flying quickly caught the world's attention. Inventors, engineers, and businesspeople were soon designing new types of airplanes and imagining new ways to use them. Today, airplanes play important roles in our lives. Worldwide, millions of people travel by air every day. Mail and packages are transported around the world by planes. Aircraft rescue people in danger and allow doctors, medicines, and supplies to reach people in need anywhere on the globe in a matter of days—or even hours.

Turning mere curiosity and dreams of flight into the amazing aircraft and spacecraft that we have today was not easy. It took a lot of testing, practice, and persistence. It also took courage. Along the way, flyers have taken many risks, and some have lost their lives in the process.

My own path "into the air" as a pilot—and later into space as an astronaut—started simply. As a child, I envied the birds and wondered what it would be like to fly something myself. Step by step, I followed my curiosity and built my skills. Flying in space was my greatest adventure and reward.

The future of flying will be built by people who dream about new types of aircraft and about new destinations in space, and then design and test and practice until they make their dreams come true. I hope you will be one of these dreamers and fliers.

Kathryn Sullivan, Ph.D.

Dr. Kathryn Sullivan, a former NASA astronaut who served on three shuttle missions, was the first American woman to walk in space. She currently serves as president and CEO of the Center of Science & Industry (COSI), a nonprofit institution based in Ohio that is dedicated to creating powerful exhibits and programs that make science learning fun.

OLD DESIGNS STILL WORK. PEOPLE TINKER WITH HOME-BUILT AIRCRAFT. HANG GLIDERS SOAR. HOT-AIR BALLOONS RIDE THE WIND. BIPLANES LOOP THE LOOP. AND DRAGON-FLIES STILL ZIGZAG THROUGH HOT SUMMER AIR.

RESOURCES

BOOKS

Dalton, Stephen. *The Miracle of Flight*. Willowdale, Ontario: Firefly Books, 1999.

Farb, Peter, and the editors of Time-Life Books. *The Insects*. Alexandria, VA: Time-Life Books, 1980.

Jablonski, Edward. *Man With Wings*. Garden City, NY: Doubleday and Company, Inc., 1980.

Jackson, Donald Dale, and the editors of Time-Life Books. *Aeronauts*. Alexandria, VA: Time-Life Books, 1981.

Lopez, Donald S. *Aviation*. New York: Prentice Hall Macmillan Company, 1995.

Moolman, Valerie, and the editors of Time-Life Books. *The Road to Kitty Hawk*. Alexandria, VA: Time-Life Books, 1980.

Moolman, Valerie, and the editors of Time-Life Books. *Women Aloft*. Alexandria, VA: Time-Life Books, 1981.

Needham, Joseph. *Science and Civilisation in China*. Vol. 4. Part 2. Cambridge: The University Press, 1965.

Peterson, Roger Tory, and the editors of *Life*. *The Birds*. New York: Time Inc., 1963.

Prendergast, Curtis, and the editors of Time-Life Books. *The First Aviators*. Alexandria, VA: Time-Life Books, 1981.

Taylor, Michael J.H., and David Mondey. *The Guinness Book of Aircraft*. London: Guinness Superlatives, Ltd., 1984.

Taylor, Michael J.H., and David Mondey. *Milestones of Flight*. London: Jane's Publishing Co., 1983.

BOOKS WRITTEN ESPECIALLY FOR YOUNG READERS

Collins, Mary. *Airborne: A Photobiography of Wilbur and Orville Wright*. Washington, DC: National Geographic, 2003.

Hockman, Hilary, editor, et al. *Planes. What's Inside Series*. New York: Dorling Kindersley, 1999.

Hunter, Ryan Ann. *Take Off!* New York: Holiday House, 2000.

Moser, Barry. *Fly! A Brief History of Flight Illustrated*. New York: Harper Collins, 1993.

Sloane, Christopher. *Feathered Dinosaurs*. Washington, DC: National Geographic, 2000.

Weiss, Harvey. *Strange and Wonderful Aircraft*. Boston: Houghton Mifflin Company, 1995.

Zimmerman, Howard. *Beyond The Dinosaurs! Sky Dragons, Sea Monsters, Mega-Mammals, and Other Prehistoric Beasts*. New York: Atheneum Books for Young Readers, 2001.

WEB SITES FOR EXPLORING FLIGHT

Build the Best Paper Airplane in the World
http://www.zurqui.com/crinfocus/paper/airplane.html

Plane Math Activities
http://www.planemath.com/activities/pmactivities4.html

Science Fun with Airplanes
http://ohioline.osu.edu/~flight/homepage.html

Wright Brothers Aeroplane Company and Museum of Pioneer Aviation
http://www.first-to-fly.com